TRIAGE

CECILY NICHOLSON

Talonbooks

Talonbooks
PO 2076, Vancouver, British Columbia, Canada V6B 3S3
www.talonbooks.com

Typeset in Benton Sans and printed and bound in Canada.
Printed on 100% post-consumer recycled paper.

First Printing: 2011

The publisher gratefully acknowledges the financial support of the Canada Council for the Arts; the Government of Canada through the Book Publishing Industry Development Program; and the Province of British Columbia through the British Columbia Arts Council and the Book Publishing Tax Credit for our publishing activities.

Library and Archives Canada Cataloguing in Publication

Nicholson, Cecily, 1974 –
  Triage / Cecily Nicholson.

Poems.
ISBN 978-0-88922-657-9

  I. Title.

PS8627.I2393T73 2011   C811'.6   C2010-907422-X

June Boag Coleman
(spring 1946–winter 2008)

Acknowledgements

This book was compiled on unceded Musqueam, Squamish and Tsleil-Waututh land.

A version of "Service" appeared in issue 6 of *Memewar* magazine and a version of the poems: "awake invertebrate," "barter," "city gothic," "Landing," "Progressive loss of vision," "pulp," "Quota today," "resolvency," "stopped" and "warm" appeared in *West Coast Line* volume 62.

–

My sincere thanks to Neil Brooks, Wayde Compton for your direct encouragement, Harsha Walia and Jeff Derksen for your thoughtful reading of my work and Steve Collis, for seeing it through.

to all of you, shoulder to shoulder.

Hannah Calder, Mercedes Eng, Ivan Drury, Press Release, Chido Johnson, Avenida Once, Larissa Lai, Urban Subjects, Ayumi Mathur, Michelle Hagenson, Daniel B., Ken and Sandra, Carol Martin, Alice Kendall and the women of DEWC.

with love, for Jef Clarke and our canoe.

Contents

COMPANY TOWN

loyal cut back strike riot tack

last outpost

copper mine

business endeavours the main thing hit
like a tonne per operated hour operating
the main thing to keep the main thing the main thing
inexpensive it takes focus – a perfect shift

back to basics is core not complex work
down events are not acceptable
down events are not normal
down events are the enemy of reliability

we triage capacity to the company
assurance town uninterrupted stability
measures sourcing productivity
engineer analysis of the appropriate

response guidance bright angel canyon
all the boats in once everyone data seems
unwell everyone appears to be dying still
don't believe in changeable rock progression

sometimes it's fallen work orders following
warrants hope you're walking chalk cursive
arteries facile supplique préolympique
free clinics make money money everything

erodes around while some people can
call keep calling rain ain't no emergency
people speak poetry others batten holed up
deep let me tell you if you've been in my shoes

brother you'd know how it is often too much
aggressive new year prices invest earn enjoy
buy on board ground private no property
stick to own kind convene containers trailers

smaller than circles swinging hammer born
for driven engines once rewarded for their steam
assembly of currency in the shadow of many things
white-knuckling through I met my first computer

plan stops to wonder more than schedules
or calculate we have all the pieces we are not
configured to use them few stars stationed over
the harbour home forgot for the fear, dear fancy

now turned blue cornflower understand we
understand reasons livable terms to liable
project reports manual and makes payroll
deduction system reset payment return clean

fine credit deduct balance balk individual
with the common touch regard sentence
fresh flower vending machine out of change
she wanders nighttimes enduring maintenance

strong earnest office there is community
salary untiring united only to the vine pinch
between thumb and index other thrashed about
las metas de hoy as day workers packers steers

incendiary tank will cause condo development
will cause mass extinction of cellular life
will cause completely safe rotating tomorrows
real a special place yes their secondhand

billion remote people retouch priorities
wealth of experience to a slow music dispersal
vibrations screw loft loose right taut authority
restrict air ways. somos un solo rio voice, voice

SERVICE

imagine a careless life

i.

partial
unlocatable
my back
these unforeseen events
return smelling of apples
new claims for capital

muddy water ways
wearied carcasses
remains netted
lines towed

small everywhere
bristling

lettered pages
long gaunt views routes
outside intent

essential in the vast winding habit trails of road agents
hurried overworked folk who cleave their way with shouts
to be shorn and unvoiced in sumptuary (coming age of) space

dust scattered light
escapes the billboard's western sky
hear the laughter glow

we all lift
delicate strands insist
our complicit
happy homes

ii.

Common techne
plural practical and flexible
nurtured on sour ground work songs
unit(ar)y hymnals ascendant grinds
swash salvaged lumber wax binder-twine
[we] drift

Taking in water
an awkward discipline

Strays gather to moult
under bridges
small dot passages to mouth

Service rids city misery

Swallow stone grit git round with risk

Rest "bod[ies] of waived matter" we are home

By powder and led we are home

Temperate bayou smelling of diesel
harbours less

Security worries less
imports offer up
grist to the mill

This was the distillery
smoking all the time like the boys
on rusted red and blue tankers

Anchored comes no closer

Coal face a victim of careless talk
giving donations

Attack on all fronts
antiquity bought
victory bonds

"gringolandia mon amour"

Income perform
corners

Prefers live-in work-in
espalier apartments

Uniform purges

State of starlight tours

Ruthless ministrations
sawtooth salt heritage
working still

Borderlines in motion
tin casings
greasy chambers

Eyes slide by eager to buy
articles for use and contemplation

Every want wins associations

Economy comely
crafting things of value

Ruinated sumpweed

iii.

Blood bugs rival roaches
pigeons rustle
meeting after meeting
bit percentages stitch in light industry
residential ground level retail
commercial activities

Blank lank dominant filters
drinking order

Rented privacy
spent in clinics

"Hold her there."

... sake, let's take you to sobriety, what a day
pain in a thin tine

No weekend after the last banner

ture of a tree. Her cure so far out of proportion
pose it was

Licensed to be used
did nothing to make it safe

On the porch step
too soon nature being ex-
plained policy modules
on dotted line joints that are ditch
sign here and here

Someday sell our roofs

Legacy of efficiencies
black dots on a white tongue
ripping shreds

"Do a snow dance" he is eleven, his mother laughs.

Sally Ann and so on sprawl across sunny peaks
playgrounds will melt

Where medicine grows children are strong

May the day break

Kind keeping six witness
vagrant years of enclosure
external mechanical influences
intensification of throughput indifference

Will work for bus tickets travel-sized toiletries socks and cigarettes

Enforceable order

Apothecarial fronts
sick back

Prospects
orange cap pop
blot land remakes survival

Indigent burials

Wardly heart
wretch surge

Memorials
bruises

Yellowed sage and blackberries
age behind the brewery

Old railway
tracks end in bramble

Broken faces living under a bridge kiss
ham drippings, salt from an old man's rags

Waning gibbous lamp low hundred block
sighing alder flats

Branches woven above mossy decay
methadrone

Bushwhacked knotted leaves
pale undersides expose
certain rain

Interrogatory hospitality
a box with good handles

iv.

unwaking
once told
the welt rose
freed her from school
the convent
east of the family lake
chromium zinc sanitizes
skins
... darling chlorintine

Opaque
loose unsalved splinters

three by seven
twenty by thirty
fifteen hundred square feet
people
in boxes
[we] will never be defeated

V.

It was a hard winter

"war again goofs everywhere"

Blind brother
an unexpected hit

Farewell day prices can't be beat
body in a lobby entrance

Removals

Holidays

Flip side: five turkey dinners two block radius

Get out

She hopes to make it to Port Coquitlam

Milagros! Construction's down

clamber music

Died revived reached for her lunch
Again for four days on the floor

People step over bodies

Reoccurs talking to the light switch
in her head without her daughter

"I will die so on"

A concave web a windshield of a yellow car
135 driver reports: transit is secure

"will is futile the pull overwhelming"

Police laugh
force three men to sit on the ground and remove their clothing

Kick her
"you can't sleep here"
already pushing a man under arrest

Rest an embattled rendezvous

Battles dense
with echoes
9/8s

Quick soft hand negotiations
Baton and boot give us hard hand
conducted energy tactics

We have a public

Frank Paul

War everywhere goof again
purges chutes and scaffolds
climbing inconstructions
written everywhere to the service

Layoffs forever Riverview
More ward property

cells
meds
grills

Love short lives late
into the daily maintenance

Get it done

Get down

Recovery wired plateaus

An end to harms

Kitchen scissor cuts
cutting in the kitchen
neatly, ugly, like skills

vi.

Husband's rent check
Welfare says it's domestic (prolly a crack thing)

Food bank's a long commercial walk
past Flowers and fresh meat
for cardboard boxes re-sealable bags

Downtown corral cows easy in the clover

Messages all teeth
mine factions

No quote photo-op
collapsing roofs

Neighbourhood groups
own nothing that can't be stolen

> *Stop the spread of disease*
> *Doesn't everyone want*
> *cleaner alleys and streets*

Remains found

Everyone seems relatively calm

Another blue bag
side of the road

Common chicory in sixteen's ditches

Hometown hands do what they can
make the phone ring

Last seen missing
posters in every slapdash shitty shelter

Surveillance architecture kneels over remnants

The house is down by two am
peers from the wreckage
Nothing in the eyes
expects to see rushing home
the cabbie speaks of fallen trees
whales leaving sea

Successive bodies
contingents of rioting hosts

In the mean volunteer streets
we need to find cover
Flicker of a thin discursive film

Unable to sit still multiplies

Beneath hospital and holding cell windows
parking lot vigils

Warrior song bodies
hushed in headlines

vii.

May it break again

Silken tethers pleasures and surety
citizens let graffiti go unchecked

2010 RIOT "you have my leye"

Alaska to Argentina
Continental stretch

Sleeker things are "imbricated"
even these days are complicit
wire runway razor-laced walls

Holes in reservoirs
Thirsty organized queues cross the threshold
Children happen and dig holes in sand

Feet blistering failures
Keep leaving the ground

Constant working back ashtrays and footrests

That last cigarette made me feel sick
finished it anyway

Nervous part of the system "our troops"

Scrape flints renew priming
Water small shot sand
whirl about the delicate

Sound opinions

Frequent visits to the mouth upgrading

Irreducibly complex but a mousetrap

No underground for these sores storeys high

Made for the night could be better could be worse

Harried passers-by comb quiet appellate streets for fresh kills
small scale tobacco

Ship chandler pubs
loggers supplies
Written on walls
mutters to mothers

Loves
sharp in the distance

Trembling fingers dig for atoms
resistance plump and blackened

HURRIED

Horizons returned inaccessible.

(K. Brathwaite)

on scale

hedge on par to capital

injection recognized as ink

reduced rates with coupons

sanctuary future fade-proof record

the day comes
when no body will handle the refuse

storage closest and bathroom floor
sleeping standards negligible

alcove acquaintance steps into a car
his car side street isolated warehouse
high ceilings and uninsulated walls

carbon bodies hardly warmed
conditioning predictable
costs and storms

baseboard heater dash slippery liquor

downturned mouths telling stories
curved belly worldly

believes her

empty can ash on the rim

increased cost of living decisions

investment attention a portion between

appropriate

Whereas therefore zoning amendments allow for existing development
to expand uses without it pre-empting overall zones review slate stand
to protect place ... les murs ont des ailes ... letters proud sponsors online
intent paper participant fees forfeited in this timely application process
software dial tones are excise consigning submit neatly and proper files
for the complete document entry system regard claims when encounter
information hour body language answer awfully dark employment rebel
populace downtown blue north metropolis special care string through air
return with receipts awake wide narrow corridor cold hard construction

take it
from my mouth

carrier

joints thicken
vertebrate self life
left fractional

multi-part message
In mime format
fabrication ltd. missions

non-participating
driver commits
drop-off and pick-up

chauffeur filigree
twisted gold
sunset hotel

back of his jacket
painted skeleton
  "my bones"
print in a factory

resolvency

Vie vole fractious o process o rhythm

tain that specular social schism il ne faut

jamais perdre le contrôle de la danse as thou

art double unanimous fixity delicious everybody

knows formation social leaves divided entities, foliage

shade presses assembly folds middle percentages faux

fur berry wine for men redneck answers fleeting clock forth

tectonic sorts resettle chest scarped gentle sloping port portals

agency acquaintance

very much like walks on fresh

air very much loves nature

like the sea is pleasant

to float in the summer

or float and sunbathe

learn you better wish

what do you think of it

names me more to like

years of me twenty-eight

therefore float and sunbathe

too a bank of lakes and grand

through me it would be desirable

and you there floating onto beaches

having valid happen as you look ahead

hopes smile awhile I finish this my letter

if interested you should then write me too

city gothic

solidarity enact steps here
unreal protocols wild essential
flows developer come dancer

discount show set multi-easy
kind of down-load-formal projet
pdf-ville ensemble shorten hems

back stage management camera
je me rêve! faster than transit
the address island outre-mer

current men evict at work he
thinks mise en sight in digital
appropriasse wig finely reddish

something stolen somewhere
distant thunder means nothing
specks flare on film pretty air

quality diversion keep an eye on
nothing superior match movement
sounds sturdy private headliner

hello so calle beat blend mild
enroulage arrangement cielo
tap tap public shipment practical

matter intervals leisure fashion
ephemeral first cause contempt
hurricane rose remix

tragic

bramble clime
compromised slip
caste porcelain
mug and saucer

innumerable states
of place territory

around the water
broken unabridged

tar baby cosmetic
bath and beauty

things you wrote

turning a shade pro-
ductive à la poursuite
d'un nuage rose years

knit fine antidote

parts

work radius

noise tries

sounds puncture
midst clutter colour

extreme curvature

"vulgar"

of course as
probably already

knees

up to no frills
silt water

seams schedule
last inseparable

notes smoker

audience ways

junk junctions
flashing lights

place looks like

coarse future
hard sale

thrill bottle green

conduction
convection

cove red
close

pending closure
closed

polished giving

strictly access

speaks pretty
peripheral lean

take sight
sit ticking

neglect wrecked
branches hurry

huzza loft
on block

conversions

confusion flood
ground

sound cut fill
and cut forges

flat road
until Rockies
yet coast

engine brakes
small towns

select spectacle

lake prow
after hours
on the radio

multiples

Undoubtedly alive eyes
granular network texture
stormy chemical solute

clasp tarnish fibre change
brocade airiness stoke fight
discipline motion dissolute hoops

playing cards rhythmic inertia
flu of all senses latent punch lines

thick them heavy
wear outstretched
arms loaded with lightening
then a quiet cloud of carbon

unfailing lightness fictitious
black spots will hurricane

lyric spatter perfume of Violet
pulsively wit yo polio playback
solitary figures solidarity figures

Quota today

Discretionary spending stops money like water finds its own level. Terms recessed divest as pirates writ slow worth. Everybody please stay calm hands shake with adrenalin – newspapers gather at the door. A caravan open angry iron ripping yarn. So serious us we are at war. I've taken some time to think

seriously to place path past daft – the take – the slanted light hitting the bevelled glass. Splayed piquant gifts plastic pouts. Glossy tips teeth enamel errors. Trial and vector errors. Our era – our beautiful then buried. The goods weren't for you of course as you were never here or hurried crow call call.

Thundering herd real economy rolls off reserves irrational flight cashing in treasury currently disposable. The rule of drudge. Output rather, outcome come income, rather input puts sources into salaries earned rent temporarily residing on his fiscal sofa. Soft expenditures grant activities lease signatories and so on. Infection certificate of good standing get your vote on Saturday. City developers' capital coordinates. Who uses who took the call from home

SHORE

information gathered as the relatively sedentary lingcod wander

Industry begun

Long ago hours induce runtime forecasting
deference per quota per lifetime lays
a blanket down it is living by a stream green
between sidewalk walk carefully here people
overwhelmingly

dirty. She'll fast no matter why decades end
bedroom barn church basement doorway
dinner plates corporate counters

As many as melodies no longer missing
flowers trees bird houses

Open end protection bunker longing ago
holds a spot a hut on flats a draught stage
catches her hair heart thumping

Recovery all around fight force my arm

Orange skies pm to pm land blasts interrupt
atmosphere productivity decay blue dot runtime

Found estuary

Unicorn public tock news evening post farmers
harrow muscle garrison

Compromise shoulder to the wall certain escape
but wii cannot speak

Spurs protrude yellow cube

Try to imagine the ringing we hands up acknowledge
hooking fingers austerity

Winged ecology poly

A field a wide cage surrounded by experts in taut survey
trace history to write pages

Movement gravely othered

Graves goods porters face front army dysphoric

Reserves hand sanitizer

What to eat at the library

Un peu de discipline et montre ta bonne mine

Move grateful memory

Departments defenders
all over country our game
plan and our operational
plan adopted as their own

wing rip. Trust no ones

All averred ones to darn down atmosphere
hear wistful signals morning along the coastline

the latest

fluttering dailies
stupid stop gaps
perverse shank

the gash is mine
is undermined

"so sorry"

clear look out
from here
to boundary

on guard/en garde
camo dreams
buildings fall

piles of creosote

ravens and rust

still water fire debris

river levels well

are we they
now looking at ether

read recently in the newspaper
lightning struck the paper mill
setting wet bales on fire

water   **front**

water	front
vane rachis quills	adding to the cart
innate song syrinx	structural economy
maintenance in stalls	road captioning
coroner informs	fallen down
harder alder [flats]	art precinct
black and white	dominoes east
sun on suits	sweet air
we they unruly	company an edifice
secure from sudden	terrible mischief

things to be done

hands put together objects collect

category directories
docile here

give over occupiers

distance vicinity

depth shallow

format good be better
view on black back ground
absent idlers on water
low branches clear

for each a warm coat after party
far from malls up clusters of happening

we'll rely on breastbone attitude
embrace as coats

staggered forms

miss transportation

idle ear to barely music

storm clouds spit other places

North slope

Perches gateway road industry wells port and trestles
bowed to fuel that precede housing facilities. Today
a rare gull sighted on shore of the north slope

–

Fell awake to the neighbour crouched by the bed
side table seeps waterway swabs dna for the record
Spilt glass when water the lamp got knocked over

–

Diamond strict seismic pipeline flows pcb room. Metal
heavy and soft room interview since an alarm had been
sounded. An arsenic cache startled sentinels heed climate

local

make relief
steady rain

wet myth specificity

matters made brier

broken downy

beneath ground
hands smell sprouting

dominant black and tan
indian stand outcries ups
outings on walls for what

ears á voix haute (across segregated sets) evict

sound motion sum of micro spark art complications
given material give arson atonal hood propped open
threshold remote heartless ecology far from useful
trauma happens quiet somatises bodies hidden

forces declined voices wound aesthetics
blind tunnel clash average sleek habitus

dig dialogical sturdy differences
do not collapse

Undo manufacture

Where care givers are

When was the design

Born bread broke
Crying in the bank

This is worth acres

Tailings long-term relations

Slightly coloured
Sections a storey

Mimics multiples

Stairs for flights
Elevator often breaks

Have-not positionality
In a rank craven mass

Why ware bootstraps pulled
While writing men with guns
You are with paper
So angry drawn wrought

Shift narrow start train to
Leased line own right of way

Nothing at all just
Natty metamaterial bruises

Blaring bodies awake

Public works
            Regulation slash
            Restoration slash
            Beautification slash
Being revitalized

Tastes to a place series

Sophisticated empathies

Landing

Paint beautiful ceiling history assumes
Empty names too labour intensive

Continuing journeys in the hold lists water
Holding cells at Elmina market place

Harmony armada gross supremacy
Temporary tents tourist information

Industry aura articles legless glory
Endures houses empty of blankets

Ordinance curfews leash law park rules
In effect no organized gathering without permit

Stirred investment due west gesture
Return empty equity bases are sameness

Static currency train creeps imperfect
Activities echo last spectre spike derail

Set afire property secure a priori
Breeding lilacs by the bloody wall

In I own exiles rotten world hate
"So callous a code as gain" undefined terminus

We detach from painted background

May your road be fulfilled
May you grow old as ritual poetry

Way points

All right ah
yawl could you
spare a quarter
from the side

We are feeling
the rising heat
of corporate risk
management

Conventional drive
motor combined
elements don't dance

Stakes pages stages
protest pens their fire
eyes nerves neurons

Function mechanical
flag flaps the mere
us fluttering monarchs
to war the updraft

We know our way

– 30 –

fine dark carbon particles
form or release during combustion

Press release

Dry rot collapses a sapling fence. Firewall or proxy –
liberation an impassioned tick. Promises electr(on)ic

music. Remote peril the coming storm. Farmers and fishermen
On my hooking mind the near rabble an earnest contingent

Milk-fed homestead to movable all the time will break you down
Components put to work. Soldiers successive bodies. Lovely you

Shoulders the shoreline at dusk. Foot-first takes a dip into cold
and unkempt past. Theirs to reach there only want me gooey. Faceless

you torso twist you waistline whittler you progress you faq map
you do not agree you see you are endless small disputes linking

Fragile commands only my questions firmly. Raise a question
and minimal. Driven by driven on pinging is thin. Plain grit

gravel road knees sets of scars. Love cold rain and came through by bus
I saw my people. This, this is the place and you will bend your back

Trouble lights keep construction lit. I keep my feathers numbered
Honest hapless sense of we are everywhere what counts as success

Storm passed; a young grandmum. Young one pregnant going on five years
now. "Yes ma'am, saw her brains and everything." Stopped

keeping track. Hardliner railings rant increases. Will we all need
distress now sweeps down the corridor. Gates hold the homeless

Obsessions gentle using to unusing pulse we know better we

aren't surprised at wave condensates overlapping crises
As waves so longer and longer overlap till the means blur

Coast home spun post. Ragged edges overlie polite measures. Brier
sub rosa summer. Standpoint constellations leave no tense nor

time for sleepers. Put systems simple wishes to rest. Everything
we've got we've got to adapt. Disorder – border an arterial clip

calibration

absolute value of a number a number without its sign

zero here dull veneer no justice no peace crisp uniforms

lax interest rates sweeping coat or cheery cipher stride

list argumentative array references audio is enchanting

attention that remains constant payments wrest incline

balance return infringes value course a bottle ensemble

rogues tightly rolled brightleaf, we're counting problems

reports the *Sun*: Rock in Whalley. ramblers push envelopes

the clowns tanked full of malevolence and loganberry wine

dispersal or restraint necessarily. hard time decision-makers

summons

Vicam Sonora México
condor confederacies

en un comunicado a los pueblos
indios de América y del mundo, celebrarse

built armament   everyday
denial the sanctity of partnerships

no item off the table substantive
pragmatic without deference to sensitivities

the contentious intractable issues
simply require time to ripen politic ally

meat and fleece "If we fail in Mexico"

bring the boats in

three hots and a cot

loss of limbs
knocking alien

look at me like that

Vision Needle: my pen
on call

outreach
promising initiatives

private sector
cares for you

benches to pews

gentle launch
centralized collateral
selection referrals

felt dirt brown
all walls white

buy now plan never

asking prices
hang heads hold bibles

promissory notes

crowd control units

what ever you like
as we do what we do to get by

highways in loving
memory surges

(young) *rust never sleeps*

Tyendinaga

gun powder merry
effigies issued widely

warrants delivery
contestable assembled

off-site trucked in daylight
hours end hauling

gravel out building in
justice to community

coffers public long live
defend delays stem

from alarm collapses
well untendered

we stormed the bridge
we beat the people

blood on the road

bystanders

Warm

Discretionary scaffolding accommodates
Authorized personnel indefinitely remote

Redding to see public notch dip each weird wheel
Worked fine on its own gravel road quirks trick

Reveal creases in sync bulging lines chromatic
Aberrations romantically addicts garish aftermath

Strong string circular circus. Top node reason pattern
Stratum dense strategy. Coming to terms with

Cannot control how I am used by proxy. Will not
if only. Standby elite is easily building stacked globes

Will survive the comments advancing
northern winters. At long lost this is not a game

Barter

orbit breaks orbit flee district actual
top of the line contrails allocate overhead

shoulders automatic hair file downy audit
end of accruals filter war warmer

climate-run by lamp rows to rose numbers
standard forms falu sangre taught army

olive liable in blue chicory junket
balance gold columns open side reset grind

well woven administrative receivables
admit lip competency as parks deposit cart

system bleak systems credit flowers release
procedure banked manual action fresh

sweet bureaucracy user friendly fee
brick walls give evening and ever apply wolf

pulp

careful motions keep body balance radial lines fiction
contractions arrive quicker thicker handles feel good

weighs in at a feather friendly wouldn't it be nice now
temporary like this pulse skipped his staccato jumped

cold water particulars consciousness-raising a mute
a collective turn north imports are off-record hung

head next hurried necks whip lash whip back lash
wanders in off boulevard around role call read first

learn the room pace partisan chemical pond relations
isotope shortage the selves out of storage wings

gnawed bleak picks pile finds things compassionate
crap taken to hone away home the exercising military

amasses hands on aircraft hovers next to the moon
swore it was a star though it never moved its unblinking

mass meetings into the gasp laugh aflutter catch
purpose "you do not have the authority to direct traffic"

Progressive loss of vision

There is no news until we gather ground
Boulevards [harbour] soldiers threat
Minor text manual leaflet infrastructure
Forecasts emission emergency preparedness
Tagging removal done economy "eyes with pain"
Boom arbitrage blast ecology non-plastic
Vertebrae clatter balance click pavement
Transfers of our time rift food security weak
Off-grid reflection ability pays principle
Falls to parts evolves to cinder
Un rest make shift before long carbon
Graphite diamond gold standard striking
Soot stifling – what do eye know – how to work
Commodity threads second hand-to-hands soft
It's often not sad actually well-shaped lass
Thread matters subtle shifty off-grid inflections
Sexy on strike hardliner amid similars he she
Felling trees landmarks up blockade-seeking
Sisters satisficing geometries turbid activities
Accrue naturally siltified flows in the true remedy

Our road
systems are obviously
critical to everything

we do, he said.

If you block
a major artery

that commerce, industry, business
and the opening
ceremonies require, you

know
the tolerance of the police
is likely

to change.

(B. Mercer)

For perfect protection

This is the unit responsible for the unit that will get us
Through 2010 strictly from an enforcement perspective
Preparatory exercise the command crime fighters farewell
Significant uniformed personnel presence affect arrests
Army accustomed to that very mixture, army their asses!

Predatory security goes deep navigation crew in the event of
Despite the magnitude of the file proceeding nicely sealed
Good liaison with those people their organizations feel that
Appropriate political and commercial expression is to be
Expectorates flu resort district relax put your feet up on
Commensurate rights to protect you our partners dictate

Amateur swastikas telling the O story attentive to fat brand
Culture clean as commercial monitor fast access and action
Local be filter for Canada is market branding tramples snow
Some archive surface gloss growth chemical barb sickening
Trump if they give up making money it will demand payments

Musical billions the spirited staples sharp through actual paper
Outburst souls strategic importance of making we must make
Special requests (special requests will not be granted) must be
Taken from cordoned traffic dividers teal-coated drivers
Lanes reserve arteries and feudal O contra la muerte, why

Eh, me hoser inarticulacy, these are the days of miracle
And wonder gather counter attach here un bout d'horizon
On the field of demonstration sporty always closing, sing

Today at tent village
(with love to the elders and organizers)

Alcatraz is not an island it's an idea
(That's Robert Oak's words)

We have to take back the land

The Russian media wants to talk to someone

I love Vancouver

I'm going to the Women's Centre

We need some reading material
We need some wood
We need some bricks

Once we unite they cannot bend us
They're not going to walk all over us

Doesn't anybody want to speak to the Russian media

Cedar and sweet grass are at the bottom of the fire, it's for peace

VANOC doesn't like fires

She's been running for two years

They went looking for me at work

You know how to talk

You're needed here

I thought it was cigarettes, but it was a pack of playing cards

Is this the tent city? This is the right one eh, there isn't another one around here?

Cheap, but it's not a cheap chair

I remember the reclamation site at Six Nations
It was barren because they had taken all the trees
I remember trying to set up my tent in that wind

airport calm

beyond the Andes

our brazen out
against invasion
night
camaraderie

unconquerably
hyper in the hyper sickness

gathered supplies

steel workers' hall

the might
steal water

state laws plan hunger

stats austere adjustment

deficit contracts truly
a national effort

obliges five metres

figurative goals
gauge standards

performing ever, we are still
human ways

not carrying weapons
to offer song

reside millennia
owners forgotten

prisons expand

      though the bee human

      love symmetry

      they are larger than holes

enclosed outer small gauge mounted on jersey barriers

expanded inner metal line flatter and even smaller gauge

jersey or anchored directly into pavement in the core

since the record began it's the hottest year

rails dig deeper into the small

of back barely possible

feet trampled

over budget forest fires

constable says she went for the gun

a record number drowning this season

Haitian hospitals reconstituted oil cap

target corners for the pane to give way quicker

know your ask contribute process growth pretends fence

SUCK CITY

elms grow sparse
black-spotted parasols

news

murders' steady streams
the afternoon sky

enroute to alder [flats]
come box stores

an old crow, right eye marred
came to rest at the back steps

feathers overlapping
barbs form jaggies

it's always March

unintelligible corvid
broken wing visible

fed it fish and bread

the end atop the storage shed

Save the receipts

No word in corporate
News of fire
The road insists
Road closures
The sidewalk fits
Our detour

Filmed arrests
Paraphernalia
Motivated violence
Fixtures hauled away
just a couple of days
1-888-JUSTICE

Weekly threat
Assessments
Time sheets
Pick pocket wallet
Weighted
Four or five figure bills

Easer to haver
Dispersal dregs
Partial proceeds
Shipped to the sticks
Tricking back lanes
Comments are closed

Social safe guard
Tents in parks
Threshold of appalling

Blues as distance

Service disturbing

Suck City

Commercial vistas

Look laws

Affect statistics

Workers overhead shout

Cheap appliances

Get your ATM here

Remand Section

over-crowded

noted tags

step by step prison

control purpose

flammable corrections

forward charges

hoodlums ware[housing]

out and out tear down

block starter refuses transfer

united form small block fires

detach dispatch instructions

kick through doors dislodge

nearly breached next block

over-capacity

double-bunked

burn building

new additions due December

August 10

earnest pedestrian

price per buildable
west of Main
as the crow flies

drum-rolled tobacco-less
cloudy over-trading
fair comparative
advantage to standing

circle committee ratio
talks with mouth full
carrier waves already
options lost open

lawyers around the world
zone multiples in systems
run by a gamut of some

not even poetry (a serious thing)

can tell by the look
talks loudly during
presentation vampires

admin for the Morning
after Vancouver
would love to have this

added to the group!

"our troops"

Cause noise

Waning crowd pales

Gears: An Urgent Message

Unmade they slowly spool

Navel radicals wrecking

The building fell

Material slid into drive-by sinkholes

A city below the street

Don't call me sweetheart

Boots get on the bus

Non-aligned nations observe

The unceded stir

Scarce cords tempered tuning

Urban sprawl consumes quiet woodlots

Surveillance we submit daily

Incorporate reserves

Fight fear distress chaos

Appear helpless

Avoid suspicion but don't look like it

Warped grid remnant bars with stages

Once the neighbourhood is gone

On my street lots aplenty

Hey there Concord Pacific!

Fails to flawlessly in crisis always

After a paycheque

Seized power resides under the table

Home is where the cart is

Accessed central came from the dirt hills

South of the Qu'Appelle

Or one of the rust bucket states

broken windows on eagle avenue

i.

months go by fireworks
lightning normal city lights
brittle Friday night February

apparent musculature
market brings in motorists

fuel and fasten seat belts passengers

traffic through the inner city skinny skirt

language sounds like choking

can't stop working

pink flower yield black-leaved thrift

dead head to keep from bolting
a part in all directions

everyone knew that hotel was a goner

overgrown with ever-bearing vines

delicious tart survivor dark

caliente deep

held by glossy hair

best in show

propagation prohibited

ordinary heat scores

pharm propaganda pro-
file a curtain open window cracked

"someone else with my name"

"a lot of spirits around me"

baseball bat forehead welt
lost the radial pulse

controlled substances up zone

great pupils attention
false eyes with many uses

read the back for more information

ii.

The Presentation Centre closing
last chance at pre-construction prices

runners make connections
board the SkyTrain without purchase

forty-storey signature properties

The Vancouver Club
The Princess League

chat choices live and local

unrushed

always new faces

cluttering echolalia
economy
a critic

acrid "critical productivity"
joy lingers

always means to say war

forces call you out

over exposure

"she ought to have earrings, long ones"

professional access

secure this door

policy probation bail
community corrections
a possible second child

awake front page
world famous
main mini mart detox

impunity
arrest this system

bingo a cross from Four Sisters

sixty-six clickety click
fifty-two thank you

greedy cough
misted pine free clinic tiles

cigs

"I'm an addict honey"

collaborative disorders

signature residences

rental office open daily

uncut hair hallways

frequenting bathrooms

luggage forgotten

neck portrait promises

plans in person

controlled premises

need to know basis

iii.

writing early morning April fourth
maths connect chromosomes
kernel of corn
taco shells imported

México
ethanol
guest workers

shaky with the fuzz

wants warrants
serve the words
so many of them mothers

across town tasers
point at persons face-down in the mud

"we're going to release the dogs"

where my shadow is the longest

consent geography

to ascent

how to make a well-heeled well-built boot
worth looking into

outdoor below in doorways
constant waiting for the number ten

purple and pink silk quilted jackets

bus passes for sale

no names
known faces

what we do with our hands

type

click this icon

iv.

spent rainy days revising

held a < / strong > < / body > social

spurious wings	(alula)
cherry blossoms	(sakura)
gold in black hills	(real estate)
arpillera	(camouflage)

snitch-jacketed aesthetics
politicked rivet

dank rummage sale season
reason walls don't meet ceiling

remote outlets
track lighting
pretty and refracted

prune back fruiting
arm spurs a tree

hickory yield
coals of distinct flavour

pictures only dark blur
of another and another and manufacture

talks between fractures

articulated buses

turn sharply catching rides

"thank you driver"

what to do with power

semi-trailing habit

end struggles

spare change

strut city murals
forget murders

Dear Gastown
paper curls @ the abdomen
variations of black paint
paint by numbers

edge of the sill still smoking kills

a road again that's where

a gaping way before

other people's density

pictures pinned to bulletins
have you seen this dog

traffic roundabout one way

fresh pitch bottleneck

Fisher-Price tour buses

v.

(calendar June)

elite beast has hourly cares
sub standards of maintenance

finally fixes a radiator leaking
black mould sopping fourth floor

three rounds of antibiotics
before they replace carpets

small claims tired after hours
cheerful talk of standing together

neon shifts up late and early
grind long stay slow

licensed ladies all-day breakfast
anytime demolition

alcoholic beverages required
to be paid for in advance

fresh sandwiches chips and candy
darts pool tables

visitors welcome beyond this point
progressive buildings

BC Collateral

"still here after all these years"

almost any cheque cashed

flip-chart paper
organized by concerned community members

attachment the great fabricator

Sunrise Market

today's special
café across from the Legion Hall

"happy birthday honey"

we coloured
quietly at the table

slight hum of a fan in the corner

a girl walks by the window

shear curtain
pink parasol

we rarely speak of elms

hard hats high viz vests and steel-toed boots

capital flow basic biometrics

winterized quarry

a wilt like this

for a century now runs quickly
behind our lovely file

satellite sincerely pressed into this moment

map future blue rubber bands
round a packet of handbills

propriety prime occasion
couth clay nation

apply

come learn about your tenancy rights
dinner provided

awake invertebrate

re-performed choke-hold five-point restraints faith-based
employment can't find a pay phone that's working late

sweet detail po-po cohere block black primed past
conducted hands police red boots decentre severe

seditious-making lesson plans little downtown
re: rallies from in alley barrels of oak flower

plant this planet commons conduct late frost loss
sugar and mineral tannic acid resources

slow leaves prime collectors metabolism fuel the gall
brown ink what's owed pollen takes to the wind

cicadas sing seventeen years waiting
to litter round the trunks spent lovers shed leaves

ripened empty seeds cold camp for acorn ants
viciously stinging workers hard hundreds of years

tunnelling signs of infestation fashion
a branch collar fastens the top button

stopped

a bell on a pole starts ringing long before you hear
narrow start train leased line owning its right of way

boyz tags to trundle on rickety unreliable
trestle bench miles of sick burners wall inhuman

wailing characters play! their roll pics raw marks
dangerous in the hold the yard ugly parts lurk

no-man's-land bang run tired starters social
affine with each anon astigmatic tread

want burn squat steal bread smash stuff love
learns schooling boxcar after boxcar run down

wrong wheel track people it is possible met
public no-name black battered skinned bods

unfurl flags fonts force our boxcar going
hit the back it's done over done some things along

the lines of this is how it is all widespread
frail ends ahead a container to sell her tells her

graf stretches three-engines on toll coaches long
in the bone tankers warehouse schedule as other

quieted alarm clang end to end up early
morning hop no more painting the side work

SHIMMER

... what would it be without birds?

(D. Brand)

i. place your body

black mesa mama day minds me
meme nive ohontsa
best don't stand in the bight
bend in the coast form an open bay

fine contraptions golden
bent wire shufflings
animated stricture
ganglia land of the sympathetic
sunset every forty-five minutes

the rest of the page stave
Staves a lake not far from here

small pond hold up in
this sickly greenback
battered manufacturing
blue steak in a two-lane truck stop

jangly fervour picture pollution
broadcast colours hum of the earth

ii. flush

a gash in the concrete staring back
capacity

since six am

signs for homes

the Empress
Columbia

"log-in, extend, live, realize"

refugee silent remains accidental

shift the mantle nano cloud

quiet & neat
cozy rooms
stop & sleep

tolerable cook and washer

they moved them and they moved them

beasts! of the notable parish

hard goods
rid surplus

empty spots

sub-prime time chicken
supple rates

food made with love

iii. patch open private

white rose hiberniate tar sand
barrel a oil per tonne a soil

wide highway Ramp is Safe

in piles of brush unidentified sparkle

capillarity ensues

full and shiny aspect

nasdaq and the dollar closed at

declining basis protect principle

retrograde pulmonary open outcry

these mast years err of provident caches
erosive last years tilt
iron laws'r'usty

emergencies on the rise

hollow state scythe staked
first flags

solidly middle class ride
up river down back roads into bars

cant in the door
suits strange angles

numbers without letters
real round assets

imperial grant handlers
evaporate product

strand board fewer exports
coastal jaw procedures do it better

eliminate open and bring in legitimate

going down nice since 64 cents

ignorant stickers on fruit

Boreal initiative
in situ projects

Cold Lake
military basis

peak punches the line through

dust mites on funny money
arterial motives

Gang Green's moratorium

Oklahoma, Houston leased our futures

guest worker

camps

pain ray whip the crowd according to plan

red next to small blue erratic

end the discussion tonight on fascism
"a man sitting by the open window, with a book"

how we become *terrorists*

how the universe became lumpy and made gears

random patch first map high resolution

material aboard a Gearbulk freighter
bound for the Atacama Desert

copper

del sulphide ore

Pan-American ways pay for pelt

iv. something should mark this place

in some light silver
Beam's *endless numbered days*

slender fingers hold
a clear plastic cup

polystyrene husk
reflects light

stale bruise
underside
left eye

makes

what
became
of the skins
iron skeleton
grills fixed on camera
wide open pane bowed brown

dirt dust dead   flies

vi. the mourning after

lichen vultures   flies
the dog who followed you up there

everyone was speechless
nothing else was alive

in the vale
bare blue strip
riches between ridges

slip of agitated rivulets
ruts

and ice droplets frozen to dust

green alpine shoal
an impervious well wicking

dampened dead pine
needle slow air

whirr to flap of wing to weight ratios
cargo

foraged plants cut young, cured by drying

threshing tinged ferment starts a fire

hearth to take the weather

gale surf snarl lip lib curl

run with care low brace breath
corner draw strokes west

vii. comely

catastrophe blooms

hillside reddens to field line
sailors delight
ocean ever in a book

sorrow's kitchen
sewn brick insulation

witnesses intersect

regime comes to

strangers hover concerned

death brings flowers

agrarian calendar wavers

crook and thumb warble

cloaca kiss machine ways
screech buteo

rhythm sounds dispersal

debris greens soil

viii. uniform

wrists thick with repetition
iron lashes

letters part general ledger

  bank (back) book
finance (real) economy

barb brain
boot blister

fieldstone masonry
passive solar energy

potbellied stove freeflow smoke cedar hair

rhythm of the chopping to the rhythm of the saw

how to hold your thumb on the fret board

viv. mines in the belly

neologistic distension
buckled

missing
years risk reading

brittle filament in sediment small
space in between could mean anything

sublimating snow from the tip of Baker
form of a cloud

nursery crusades
nouns dream

to augment mutual reins

our lucky era riven with circuitry
self-incompatibility

run to the docks
obligatory reaches agile replies

hard water stained basalt cinder
cedar stand on crystal quarry

starling plain piers unprotected
query an open sleep of surgery

ix. hard past the gate

longing for corn rows path back to scrub brush

furrowed till rust on tassels told us

combine season

rotating blades that could not hear or see

in the harvest black currants a quart an hour

the river road

through squares raw buckwheat

wildflower to a power cardboard container

x. social

we are functional by any means
uneasy associations heat the place

publicly above the din

bleak double quotes empty text

banner strip
pyrex pipe lugs

atmosphere slips park after dark

seeping plume network nodes
long tails against verticals

string unprintable

xi. rock takes flight

feathery wires grow round
our off by heart flutter

watery mothers in our mouths

cement arm symptoms
of harsh bright violent listening

modified limbs linked

ink
sky

black blooming

pitch instants inured

kanohi kitea

evening finally

copper shimmer over staccato murmur
silhouette bodies of great blues

whole for a part as the smiling year for spring
water is something

herons aswath the path

leaves me branches

xii.

partial
embattled

hearts round like family

epaulets on shoulders

aggregately owned

flyovers wreath new zest
hors de combat split upon the cord

small gangs goodly numbers

plumage splendid
seldom brought to the ground